JOHN STRELECKY

The Cafe on the Edge of the World

A Story About the Meaning of Life

Other Works by John Strelecky

The Big Five for Life

The Big Five for Life - Continued

Life Safari

Ahas! - Moments of Inspired Thought

What I've Learned - Reflections on Living a Fulfilled Life

Printed in the United States of America.

Publication Data

Strelecky, John
   The Cafe on the Edge of the World / John Strelecky.
   1st Aspen Light Publishing ed.

       p. m.

    ISBN-13: 978-0-9913920-5-6

Published by Aspen Light Publishing

Inquiries to the author can be directed to:

13506 Summerport Village Parkway Suite 155
Windermere, FL 34786

The author can also be reached through
www.johnstrelecky.com

To Casey, Mike, and Anne

Preface

Sometimes when you least expect it, and perhaps most need it, you find yourself in a new place, with new people, and you learn new things. That happened to me one night on a dark, lonely stretch of road.

In retrospect, my situation at that moment was symbolic of my life at that time. Just as I was lost on the road, I was lost in life as well—unsure of exactly where I was going or why I was moving in that direction.

I'd taken a week off from my job. My goal was to get away from everything associated with work. It wasn't that my job was terrible. Sure, it had its frustrating aspects. More than anything though was that most days I found myself wondering if there wasn't supposed to be more to life than spending ten to twelve hours per day working in a cubicle.

The main point of which appeared to be a potential promotion to then work twelve to fourteen hours per day in an office.

During high school I'd prepared for college. In college I'd prepared for the work world. Since then I'd spent my time working my way up in the company where I was employed. Now I was questioning whether the people who helped direct me along those paths, were simply repeating to me what someone had repeated to them in their lives.

It wasn't bad advice really, but it wasn't particularly fulfilling advice either. More and more I felt like I was busy trading my life for money, and it no longer seemed like such a good trade.

That uncertain state of mind is where I was mentally when I found "The Cafe of Questions." When I've related this story to others, they've used terms like "mystical" and "Twilight Zone-ish." The latter a reference to an old television program where people would show up in places that at first glance seemed normal, but didn't always end up that way.

Sometimes, just for an instant, I catch myself wondering if my experience at the cafe *was* real. When that happens, I go into my desk drawer at home, pull out the menu Casey gave me, and read the message she wrote. It reminds me of just how real everything was.

I've never tried to retrace my steps and find the cafe again. Some small part of me likes to believe no matter how real the evening was, even if I could go back to the exact spot where I originally found the cafe, it wouldn't be there. That the only reason I found it was because at that moment, on that night, I needed to find it. And for that reason alone, it existed.

Maybe someday I will try to go back. Or maybe some night I'll just find myself in front of it again. Then I can go inside and tell Casey, Mike, and Anne, how that night in the cafe changed my life. How the questions they exposed me to have resulted in thoughts and discoveries beyond anything I'd imagined before then.

Who knows. Perhaps on that night I'll spend the evening talking to someone else who *also* got lost and wandered into "The Cafe of Questions."

Or maybe I'll just write a book about my experience, and let that be part of my contribution to what the cafe is all about.

One

I was creeping along the interstate at a pace that made walking look like a high speed car race. After an hour of slowly inching along, traffic came to a complete standstill. I hit the scan button on my radio and searched for any sign of intelligent life. There was nothing.

When twenty minutes passed without anyone moving forward, people started to get out of their cars. This didn't actually accomplish anything, but at least we could all complain to someone outside of our own automobile, which was a nice change of pace.

The owner of the minivan in front of me kept repeating that his reservation was going to be cancelled if he didn't get to his hotel by six o'clock. The woman in the convertible on my left was complaining about the inefficiencies of the entire roadway system. Behind me, a carload of youth league baseball players was driving their chaperone to the brink of her sanity. I could almost hear her thinking that this was the last time she ever volunteered for anything. Basically, I was a small piece of one long ribbon of discontent.

Finally, after another twenty-five minutes without any signs of forward movement, a police car came driving down the grass center median. Every few hundred feet the car would stop, presumably to let people know what was going on.

"For the sake of that officer," I thought, "I hope they carry riot gear."

With eager anticipation, we all awaited our turn. When the officer finally arrived at our section of the highway, she told us a tanker with potentially toxic materials had overturned about five miles ahead. The road was completely shut down. She explained that our options were to turn around and try an alternate route—although there really wasn't one—or to wait out the cleanup efforts. Those would probably take another hour.

I watched the officer move down to the next group of disconsolate drivers. When the guy with the minivan twice more repeated his concerns about his six o'clock reservation, I decided my patience had run out.

"This is exactly the kind of thing that always

seems to happen when I'm trying to get away for a while," I mumbled to myself.

I explained to my new friends, that I had reached my frustration limit and was going to try a different way. After one more comment about his six o'clock reservation, the minivan owner cleared a path for me, and I crossed the grass median. Then I began heading in a new direction.

Two

I turned on my phone and pulled up the map feature it offered. "System unavailable," was all that kept showing on the screen.

As I headed south, knowing I should be heading north, my frustration built. Five miles without an exit became ten, then twenty, then twenty-five miles.

"And by the time I find an exit it won't really matter, since I have no idea how to get where I want to go," I said out loud to myself. A perfect demonstration of my further degenerating state of mind.

Finally, at mile twenty-eight, an exit appeared.

"This just isn't possible," I thought to myself as I pulled to the top of the ramp. "I'm at the one place in probably the entire world that doesn't have a gas station, a fast-food restaurant, or anything else at a highway intersection." I looked to my left. There was nothing. The view to the right was equally empty.

"Well," I said, "it doesn't look like it matters which way I go."

I turned right, mentally noting I was now going west, and at the next promising intersection I should turn right again. That way I would at least be heading back north. The road was two lanes, one taking me farther from where I'd come, the other taking me back. I really wasn't sure which one I should be on.

Traffic was very light. Signs of civilization were even lighter. I saw an occasional house, some family farms, and then nothing but woods and grassland.

An hour later I was officially lost. The only intersections I'd passed were small and marked with the type of signs that immediately indicate you're in trouble. When you haven't seen another person for forty miles, and the road you're on has a name that starts with the word "Old," as in "Old Route 65," things are looking pretty bleak.

At the next intersection, which was really no more major than any of the other intersections I'd driven by, I turned right. It was an act of desperation. At least I'd be going in the right compass direction, even if I had no idea where I was. To my dismay, the name of this road also started with "Old."

Three

An hour later, the sun was rapidly sinking lower on the horizon. As the day wound down, my frustration continued to rise.

"I should have just stayed on the expressway," I said in anger. "I was so upset about losing an hour, and now I've wasted two, and still have no idea where the hell I am."

I punched the roof of my car, as if the car had anything to do with the situation, or as if that would help.

Ten, fifteen, twenty more miles, and there was still nothing. I now had less than half a tank of gas. As far as I could tell, going back was no longer an option. With my remaining fuel, I couldn't return to where I'd started, assuming I could even find that place. Even if I made it back, there hadn't been a gas station along the entire route anyway.

My only choice was to plod on and hope I finally found someplace where I could fill up and get some food. My frustration level continued to go in the opposite direction of the fuel gauge.

I was on the trip to *avoid* frustration. I had plenty of that back home with my job, bills, and to some degree with life in general. I didn't need it here, too. This was supposed to be my chance to relax and "recharge my batteries."

"What an odd phrase," I thought to myself. "Recharge my batteries. Burn out, recharge, burn out, recharge…. How is that moving in a positive direction?"

Another twenty minutes passed and the sun had sunk completely below the tree line. Dusk was steadily enveloping the countryside. Traces of pink and orange on the clouds reflected the last essence of daylight, although I barely noticed the sky as I focused on the road and my worsening situation. There was still no sign of any people.

I glanced down at the gas gauge again. "Less than a quarter tank and falling," I said out loud.

The last time I'd slept in my car was driving back from college. That was years ago and I hadn't really planned on re-creating the event. Unfortunately, it looked like that was becoming more and more likely.

"I'll need my sleep," I thought, "so I'll have

enough strength to walk for help once the car runs out of gas."

Four

It was when the needle on the fuel gauge just started to slip below empty, that I saw the light. Seized by the stupidity of my situation, I'd taken a left turn at an intersection a few miles back. There was no indication my chances of finding anyone were going to be better by taking that turn, but I'd done it anyway. It was at least a road whose name didn't start with the word "Old," had been my justification at the time.

"An act of desperation that apparently might pay off," I said out loud.

As I got closer to the light, I could see it was a streetlight. A single, white streetlight, shining brightly in a location so remote, that it was in the *middle* of the middle of nowhere.

"Please be something there," I repeated in mantra-like fashion as I drove the quarter of a mile toward it. And sure enough, there was something.

At the light, I pulled off the road and into a dirt and gravel parking lot. To my amazement, in front of me was a small, white, rectangular building. The name *The Cafe of Questions* was spelled out in light-blue neon on the roof. Equally surprising were the other cars in the parking lot.

"Wherever they came from, it must not be the same place I did," I thought. "I haven't seen a single person the last two hours."

I climbed out of the car and stretched my arms over my head a few times to clear the stiffness from my body. "Hopefully they know something I don't about getting out of wherever it is I am," I said to myself.

I walked toward the entrance. The sky was black, except for a large crescent moon and thousands of stars. As I opened the door to the cafe, small bells attached to the inner doorknob announced my arrival.

To my surprise, a wave of appetizing aromas washed over me as I stepped inside. I hadn't realized just how hungry I was until right then.

"I don't know what they're making," I thought, "but I'm getting three orders of whatever it is."

Five

Inside, the cafe had the feel of an old diner. Chrome-colored soda fountain stools, with red cushioned tops, were lined up under a long, thin, white counter. Under the front windows was a sequence of red booths with tables in-between them. On the tables were glass container of sugar, a small silver pitcher of what I assumed was milk for coffee, and matching salt and pepper shakers.

An old cash register sat on a stand near the door. Next to it was a wooden coat rack. The cafe felt comfortable. It was the kind of place where you could sit and talk for a long time with friends. Unfortunately, I hadn't brought any of those with me.

A waitress stopped talking to a couple in one of the far booths. She smiled at me and said, "Open seating, park it where you want it."

I did my best to calm the still-simmering frustrations that had built up during my drive and attempted to smile back. Then I chose a booth near the door. As I slid onto the red vinyl seat, I noticed how new it looked. I turned and looked around and was surprised at how new *everything* looked.

"The owner must be anticipating some huge urban growth," I thought, "to build a new cafe out here in the middle of nowhere."

"Hi there," interrupted my reflections on inexpensive real estate prices and housing development opportunities. It was the waitress. "My name's Casey. How are you?"

I looked at her, "Hi, Casey. I'm John, and I'm a little lost."

"Yes you are, John," she replied with a mischievous smile.

From the way she said it, I couldn't tell if she was affirming that I was John, or that I was lost.

"Why are you here, John?" she asked.

I paused for a moment, "Well, I was going along and ran into some problems. When I tried to work my way around them, I ended up getting pretty lost. In the process, I just about ran out of gas and almost starved to death."

Casey smiled her same mischievous smile as I finished my diatribe of frustration.

"I'll tell you what," she said. "I'm sure we can help you avoid the starvation problem. As far as the rest is concerned, we'll just have to see."

She reached over, took a menu from the holder by the front door, and handed it to me. I wasn't sure if it was the light, or my fatigue from driving for so long, but I could have sworn the letters on the menu dissolved and reappeared as I looked at them.

"I must be really tired," I thought, and put the menu on the table.

Casey pulled a small order pad out of her pocket. "Why don't I get you something to drink while you look at the menu."

I ordered a glass of water with lemon, and she left to get it for me.

This day was shaping up to be much more than I'd bargained for. First a multi-hour drive through the middle of nothing, then a cafe on the edge of the world, and now a waitress with a mischievous smile. I picked up the menu from the table and read the front cover.

"Welcome to The Cafe of Questions" was on the top half of the page. Underneath, in small black letters, it said, "Prior to ordering, please consult with our wait staff about what your time here could mean."

"I hope it means I'll be getting something good

to eat," I thought to myself as I flipped open the front cover.

Inside, the menu contained the usual assortment of cafe food. Breakfast items were listed on the left near the top; sandwiches on the bottom left; appetizers and salads on the upper right, and entrees were below that. The surprise came when I turned the menu over. On the back cover were three questions under the heading—Items to Ponder While You Wait:

Why are you here?

Do you fear death?

Are you fulfilled?

"Not exactly like a glance through the latest sports news," I thought to myself. I was about to re-read the three questions when Casey came back with my water.

"Finding everything all right?" she asked.

I motioned to the three questions and then to the name of the cafe.

"What does all this mean?"

"Oh, everyone seems to have their own interpretations of that," she replied mysteriously. "Now, what can I get for you?"

I wasn't ready to order. As a matter of fact, I was a little tempted to reach for my jacket and leave. There was definitely something different about this place, and I wasn't convinced it was different in a good sort of way.

So I stalled. "Sorry, Casey. I uh…I'm going to need a little bit longer."

She smiled and shrugged, "Okay. You take your time, and I'll come check on you in a few minutes." She turned away, paused, then turned back to me. "And John," she said and smiled again, "relax. You're in good hands here."

Six

I watched as Casey walked over to the couple in the booth at the other end of the cafe. When she arrived, the three of them started talking. Whatever it was they were discussing must have been good, because within moments they were smiling and laughing.

"Maybe I should have some of what they're having," I said to myself.

I sighed and looked around. "There's no other options," I thought. "I'm about out of gas. There were no other food places for the last two hundred miles. And although this place seems a little odd, nothing too unusual has actually happened—yet."

That calmed me a little. My concerns evaporated even further a few minutes later. Casey had left the other table and gone to the kitchen. Now she was walking past me carrying two plates of pie.

"Strawberry-rhubarb," she commented as she

passed, noticing me eyeing what was on the plates. "Best around. Factor that into your ordering."

"Hmm," I replied in surprise. Strawberry-rhubarb pie was my absolute favorite when I was a kid. Hardly anyone makes it, and it had been years since I'd had any.

"Maybe it's a sign I should stick around for a while," I thought.

I looked at the menu again. Strange questions aside, the food items looked good. I decided on the breakfast platter, even though the standard breakfast hours had ended long ago. I glanced up, but Casey was talking to the couple. So with my decision made, I turned the menu over to the back again.

Why are you here?

It seemed like a strange question to be asking your customer. Shouldn't the owner already know why someone's in their restaurant? Shouldn't people eating at the restaurant know why they're there?

Why are you here?

Casey's return broke me out of my thoughts.

"Are you ready?" she asked with a smile.

I was about to reply yes, but then I remembered the message from the front of the menu about consulting with the wait staff prior to ordering. "I think so," I replied and then pointed at the message. "What exactly do I need to ask you about?"

"Oh that," she replied, and smiled again.

I was getting to really like it when she smiled.

"Over the years we've noticed people seem to feel different after they spend some time here," she continued. "So now we try to ease them into the whole 'Why are you here?' experience. We share with them a little of what they might expect, in case they aren't quite ready for what they originally thought they could handle."

"Huh?" was all my brain could register from that. I had no idea what she meant. Was she talking about food, the cafe itself, something completely different...?

"If you'd like," she said, "I can bring your order to the cook and get his opinion on what might be best."

"Uh, sure?" I replied hesitantly, feeling even more confused. "I guess so." I pointed at the menu, "I'd like the breakfast platter. I know it isn't breakfast time anymore. Is it still alright to order that?"

"Is that what you want?" she asked.

I nodded.

"Then I'm sure it won't be a problem. After all, it's closer to breakfast tomorrow than to lunch today."

I glanced at my watch. "That's an interesting way to look at it," I said.

Casey shrugged, "Sometimes it helps to look at things from a different perspective."

Seven

Casey approached the order window for the kitchen and for the first time, I realized there was a man back there. He had a wooden serving spoon in one hand and looked to be the cook. When Casey reached the window, she said something to him. He looked out at me and saw I was looking in his direction. Then he smiled and waved.

I hesitantly waved back, feeling kind of ridiculous. I don't make a habit of waving to cooks in cafes. Casey and the man continued talking, so I returned my attention to the menu. A few moments later, as I was rereading the first question—*"Why are you here?"*—Casey came back and sat down across from me.

"That's Mike," she said. "He owns this place and does all the cooking. He said he'll come out and meet you when he has a chance. I asked him about your order. He said it will be a lot, but he thinks you can handle it."

I nodded, not really sure how to respond to that. "Thanks. That's uh…, some kind of service."

She smiled, "We do our best." She reached over, picked up the menu I'd been looking at and turned it to the front. "One more thing about this," she said and pointed to where it referred to asking the wait staff. "It relates to that first question you keep reading." She flipped the menu over again, putting it back on the table with the questions facing me.

I wasn't sure how she knew I'd been reading the question, and I didn't reply.

"You see," she continued, "it's one thing to look at it. It's another to alter it."

I looked at her, confused, "What do you mean, alter it?"

"It sounds simple, as if it would have no impact," she said. "But if you modify just a few letters in that question, it changes things."

"Changes things?" I replied hesitantly. "Like what? I won't be able to eat here? Or I'll have to order something different?"

"No," she replied, slowly shaking her head, "bigger changes."

I didn't know if it was what she said, or the intensity of her voice, but at "*bigger changes*," goosebumps rose up on my arms. And while I had no idea what she was talking about, she clearly wasn't kidding around.

"I'm not sure I follow you," I said.

Casey pointed to the menu again. "If you change the question from something you ask someone else, and instead make it something you ask *yourself*— you'll no longer be the same person."

"What?" I thought. "*No longer be the same person? What the heck did that mean?*"

Suddenly, a strange sensation come over me. Like I was standing precariously close to the edge of a very steep cliff, and that if I took one step forward it would bring either immediate death, or eternal happiness.

"It's kind of like that," Casey commented. Then she smiled, "But not so drastic."

Before I could ask how she knew what I was thinking, she said, "How about if I show you, without you having to take the step?"

She motioned toward the menu. "Read the first question, but read it in the detached way you might glance at a sign as you walk past it."

I looked at her, confused.

"Go ahead," she said.

I briefly looked down at the menu. To my surprise, the question slowly transformed from *"Why are you here?"* to *"Why am I here?"*

33

As soon as I finished reading it, the question changed back.

I looked at Casey, then at the menu, then at Casey again. "Did you see…?" I began. "Did the menu just…? How did that happen?"

"I'm not sure you're ready for that answer," she replied.

"What do you mean?" I asked, my voice raising a little. I looked at the menu again, then once more at Casey. "Was it you? Did you make the writing change, somehow?"

I was totally confused with what was going on and not sure it was a good idea to stick around and figure it out.

Casey looked at me, unfazed. "John, did you see what the text on the menu turned into?"

"Yeah. It was one thing when I first looked at it, then it changed *on it's own*, and now it's back to what it started as. Why? And how?"

Casey paused, "It's like this, John," she began. "The question you saw, the one that was different—"

"The one that said, 'Why am I here?'" I interrupted.

She nodded calmly, "Yes, that one. It's not a question to be taken lightly. To glance at it is one thing. But when you go beyond glancing and actually see it, and then truly ask it of yourself—your world

34

changes."

She picked up the menu, turned it over, and pointed to where the "Prior to ordering..." was printed.

"I know that sounds drastic. Which is why we put this message on the front of the menu."

Eight

As I sat there looking at her, I was struck by the ludicrousness of my whole situation. I was in a cafe, in the middle of the night, in the middle of nowhere, hearing about messages put on the front of menus to help customers deal with their *worlds changing!*

This was definitely not your typical start to a vacation. And little did I know, it was just the beginning of what the evening held in store for me.

Casey seemed unfazed by my confusion. "You see John, once you truly ask the question you saw, seeking the answer will become part of your being. You'll find yourself waking up with it first thing in the morning, and having it constantly flash through your mind during the day. Although you may not remember it, you'll be thinking about the question while you sleep, too."

She paused a moment, "It's a little like a gateway.

Once you open it up, it beckons you."

I looked at her incredulously, "A gateway?"

She nodded, and her voice became more intense again, "And once open, it's *very* hard to close."

I sat back in my seat, trying to process even a portion of what she was telling me, or why. Gateways, parts of my being, beckoning voices…. I really had no idea what she was talking about.

One thing *was* definitely clear, though. The *"Why are you here?"* question on the menu, had a much deeper intention than I'd thought when I first read it. Obviously it wasn't just asking why someone was in the cafe.

"That's correct," Casey said, interrupting my thoughts. "It's not about the cafe. It's asking why someone exists—*at all*."

I looked around, feeling stunned and even more confused. *"What kind of place is this?"* I wondered.

My eyes settled on Casey's, but she just smiled, shrugged, and didn't say anything more. I tried to pull myself together. "Listen Casey, thank you for telling me all…that. It's uh, very nice of you. But, I just came here for some food. That's it."

"Really? she asked.

"I'm pretty sure," I replied slowly.

She just nodded in response.

"Besides," I said, trying to fill the uncomfortable

silence, "it sounds like asking that question comes with a lot of consequences. Maybe it's better to just leave that one alone. You know," I added, "because of the 'gateways' and 'things constantly flashing through your mind....'"

Casey just continued to look at me. Not speaking.

"I'm not sure why anyone would ask it, actually," I hurtled ahead. "I mean, I've never asked it and I'm fine."

Casey glanced down at the menu, then back at me. "Are you?" she asked, finally breaking her silence. "Are you really *fine*?" She said the word "fine" with a friendly bit of mockery, as if teasing me to define it. "Many people are *fine*. But some seek something more fulfilling than fine, something greater."

"And so they come to *The Cafe of Questions*?" I asked sarcastically.

"Some of them do," she replied in a soft, calm voice. "Is that why you're here?"

I was taken aback and didn't know how to answer her question. I wasn't sure *what* I was doing here. I wasn't even sure I knew what this place was.

If I were being totally honest with myself, I'd admit that for years I'd been wondering if there wasn't more to life than what I already knew. It wasn't that life was bad. Sure it was frustrating at times, particularly lately. But I had a decent job and good friends. Life *was* fine, even good.

Still, in the back of my mind was this feeling I couldn't quite explain.

"That feeling is what inspires people to ask the question you saw," Casey interjected.

Her comment caught me off guard. It wasn't just that she seemed to have read my thoughts again, although that alone was very disconcerting. It was the sensation I felt, that she might be right.

I took a long, slow breath. The steep cliff feeling from earlier was washing over me again. Something told me to take a peek over the edge. "OK," I said hesitantly, "so what else is there to know about that question?"

Nine

Casey smiled and nodded slowly, "Well, like I said earlier, asking it opens up a gateway of sorts. The person's mind, soul, or however you choose to define it, will want to figure out the answer. Until that happens, the question will live at the forefront of their existence."

I looked at her confused, "Are you saying once someone asks themselves 'Why am I here?' that's all they can think about?"

She shook her head, "Not exactly. There are some who glance at it, even see it, and then forget about it." She hesitated, "But for those who ask the question and on some level truly want to know the answer—ignoring it becomes very difficult."

I paused and tried to process that, then decided to peek even further over the edge of the cliff. "And if someone asks the question and then finds the answer?" I asked. "What then?"

Casey smiled, "Well, that's the good news *and* the challenging news."

"OK," I replied hesitantly.

She leaned forward a little, "Like I mentioned, asking the question creates the drive to seek out the answer. Once someone finds the answer, an equally powerful force emerges. You see, once a person knows why they're here, why they exist, their very reason for being alive—they'll want to fulfill that reason.

"Think of it like seeing where the X is on a treasure map. Once you know where the X is, it's harder to ignore the treasure. It's harder to not go after it. In this case, once someone knows why they're here, it's emotionally and even physically more difficult to not fulfill the reason."

I sat back again, trying to understand what Casey was saying. "So it could actually make things worse," I replied after a moment. "Like I said before, a person might be better off never asking the question. They could just go on as they have been and keep the genie in the bottle, so to speak."

She looked at me and nodded, "Some people choose that. It's something each person, when they get to that point, must decide for themselves."

I sat silently for a few moments, unsure how to respond. My mind flashed back to being in the car.

How excited I'd been to finally see the light when I was lost. Now I wasn't so sure.

"This is kind of a lot to process," I finally said.

Casey nodded and smiled, "You know that feeling you had earlier? It isn't something you can be told or have dictated to you. And if at any time you decide to walk away from it, the choice will be yours and only yours."

We sat in silence for a moment. "Speaking of walking away…," Casey added and got up from the table. "Time to check on how your breakfast special is doing."

With all the intensity of our discussion, I'd almost forgotten about the food I ordered. Casey's comment brought me back to the realization I was still in a cafe, and still starving.

Ten

As I watched Casey head to the kitchen, I found my mind spinning. I looked down at the menu and re-read the first question.

Why are you here?

It had a whole different meaning now compared to the first time I'd read it. I tried to remember the exact words Casey used. *It's asking why someone exists at all.*

On a level I couldn't quite explain, I felt like something was pulling me to ask what I'd seen that question morph into. I remembered what it was.

Why am I here?

I also remembered Casey's comments about what might happen if I did that. The possible ramifications.

I looked up from the menu and rubbed my eyes. "This is ridiculous," I said to myself after a moment. I picked up my water glass and looked through the window at the darkness beyond the cafe parking lot. "I mean, what am I doing? I just need some food, a little gasoline, and a place to crash for a few hours. That's all."

I turned back and looked for Casey. She wasn't at the far end of the cafe where the other people were sitting. When I turned to my right to see if she was at the cash register, I realized Mike was standing inches from my table, holding a pitcher of water.

"Can I give you a refill?" he asked. "You look like you might be ready for a little more."

I almost dropped my glass in surprise. He *had not* been there a second earlier. I managed to recover enough to reply, "Uh, sure."

"My name is Mike," he said as he filled my clear tumbler.

I nodded, trying to pull myself together. *How had he walked over to my table without me hearing a thing?* "Nice to meet you, Mike. I'm John."

Mike smiled, "You okay, John? It seemed like you were pretty deep in thought when I walked over."

"Uh…yeah. Something like that," I replied.

"You sure you're alright?" he asked, looking at me more closely.

Without really knowing what else to say, I picked up the menu and turned it to the front. "Casey was explaining to me what the text on the front of your menu means," I sort of stammered. "I uh, I was trying to sort it out and see if it means anything for me."

The words were barely out of my mouth and I realized how strange they sounded. Mike didn't seem surprised at all through.

He nodded, "Yeah, that's a tough one. People face it at all different times. Some sort it out when they're little kids, some when they're older, and other people never do." He paused, "It's funny that way."

Mike had a very calm presence to him. He struck me as someone who had been around the world a few times and come out on the other side of it with some major life wisdom. It felt odd to sense that, since I'd just met him. But then again, the entire cafe seemed odd.

I hesitated a moment, unsure where to go with the conversation.

Mike reached down and flipped the menu back over. He smiled, "And how's it going with these?"

"OK," I replied slowly.

"But you were sort of wondering…?" he asked.

I paused. "What the heck," I thought after a moment. "Might as well ask."

"Well, Casey explained to me a little bit about what happens if someone asks themselves a personal version of this," I said, and pointed to the first question on the menu.

He nodded in reply, seemingly unfazed by the direction I was going with the conversation.

"And?"

"And I guess part of me was wondering what they do after that?" I replied.

Mike nodded, "You mean after they ask the question, or after they find the answer?"

I looked at him, uncertain. "Both, I guess," I replied hesitantly. "Casey and I didn't get too far in our conversation. She just explained a little about what it would be like once someone asked the question."

Mike nodded again, "Well, as far as how to find the answer, I don't think there is just one method that works for everyone. We all approach life in our own way."

He paused, "If you want though, I can tell you some of the techniques used by people I know who have found *their* answer."

I thought about replying, but didn't. I had a hunch having insight into finding the answer to the question, might make it even harder to not ask it.

"That's true," Mike commented. "Same theory as Casey probably explained to you."

"Great," I thought to myself. "Apparently he too can read people's minds."

I wasn't sure I wanted him to tell me what other people had done. After all, I wasn't even sure I wanted anything to do with the question.

"How about the other piece?" I asked, trying to stall and change the direction of the conversation. "What does someone do once they know their answer to the question?"

Mike looked at me a moment and smiled. "I'll tell you what, I have a hunch your order might be almost ready. Let me go check on that. It's important everything happens…at the right time."

I looked at him, confused.

"You know," he continued. "Wouldn't want anything from your order to cook too fast or get overdone."

I nodded, as if I understood what he was talking about.

As he walked away, I took a breath and exhaled slowly. At least the stalling had worked.

Mike went to the kitchen and a few moments later returned with a tray full of plates. "Is that all mine?" I asked, wondering what two paragraph description about my food I'd missed on the menu.

He nodded, "Absolutely. One breakfast platter, complete with omelet, toast, ham, bacon, fresh fruit, hash browns, biscuits, and a side of pancakes."

I looked around to see if there were two or three

other people interested in joining me.

Mike motioned toward a group of small jars and containers on one side of the tray. "In addition to that, we've got jelly for the toast, syrup for the pancakes, honey for the biscuits, and our special tomato salsa for the omelet." He smiled, "I'm glad you're hungry."

"I'm not sure anyone is this hungry," I replied, looking at all the food.

He smiled again and shrugged, "You'd be surprised, John. Sometimes you just don't know how ready you are for something filling."

Mike put all the items from the tray onto my table, then looked at me. "John, I need to go talk with the couple at the other end of the cafe for a little bit. If you'd like, I'll come back in a little while and we can continue our conversation then if that's okay with you."

I looked at all the plates in front of me. "Sure," I replied, "no problem."

Eleven

I was halfway through the omelet, toast and fruit, when Casey came by.

"How are you doing, John?"

I finished chewing the bite I'd just put in my mouth, "I'm good. Really good, actually. This food is amazing."

"You seem in better spirits."

I was in better spirits. The feelings of frustration that had been overwhelming me when I'd first come into the cafe had almost entirely disappeared.

"Would you like to finish your meal alone, or do you prefer some company?" Casey asked.

"Company," I replied. "Definitely company." I paused a moment and then said a little hesitantly, "I'd kind of like to continue the discussion we were having earlier, actually. I've been thinking about it while I've been sitting here, and I've got a few questions."

Casey smiled and slid into the booth across from me, "OK."

I reached over to the menu at the far end of the table and slid it between us. "Well, it's about these," I said and pointed to the questions. "Suppose someone asks themselves why they're here, and eventually they figure out the reason…." I hesitated, "Then what?"

Casey paused for a few moments, "First of all, they can do whatever they want with that knowledge. They uncovered it, and it belongs to them. They have ultimate and total say about what happens next."

She looked at me, "What do you think they should do?"

I thought for a moment, "I suppose if someone figured out the reason they're here, they'd want to take steps to fulfill that reason. I'm just not sure how they'd do that."

I looked at Casey and got the impression she knew something, but was waiting for me to figure it out on my own.

"It's an individual thing," she said after a moment.

I looked at her, "How about a hint?"

"Perhaps an example would be helpful," she replied. "Suppose you wanted to become an artist in your spare time. What type of art would you create?"

I thought for a moment, "I don't know. I suppose

it would depend on the type of artist I wanted to be. I guess I'd just create whatever I wanted."

I stopped and waited for her to comment. She didn't, so I thought through my answer.

"Is it that simple?" I asked. "Once someone knows why they're here, they do whatever they want that fulfills their reason?"

As I said the words, I felt a sense of excitement race through my body. It was like I'd just found something out that was unique and important, and my body was confirming it. It sounded so basic I thought maybe it was too basic to be true. *Do whatever you want that fulfills the reason why you're here.*

"So, if the reason I'm here is to help people, then I should do whatever I want that fits my definition of helping people?" I asked excitedly, warming to the concept.

"Correct," Casey replied. "If your definition of helping people means joining the medical profession, do that. If it means building shelters in an impoverished area, do that. Maybe you feel becoming an accountant and assisting people with their taxes is the way you want to help. Then do that."

My mind was spinning a little. I'd never really thought of life in this context before. Most of my decisions had been made in response to things like family advice, cultural pressures, people's opinions and other things. This was very different.

"So what if I'm here to experience what it's like to be a millionaire?" I asked.

"Then you should do whatever fits your definition of 'be a millionaire,'" Casey replied. "If that means interacting with millionaires, do that. If it means working until you have a million dollars, do that. Just like in the other examples, the choice is always yours."

"*Be a millionaire…*" I said, getting more and more excited. "I kind of like the sound of that. I could buy a few new cars, maybe a couple of houses…"

Casey's voice became quiet. "All of which is fine," she said. "Except, is that why you're here?"

Her question caused my mind to stop spinning. "I don't know."

Casey nodded, "Mike and I have a little acronym we use. It relates to the question you saw briefly when we were talking before."

I glanced down at the menu.

Why are you here?

I watched in amazement as it transformed to *Why am I here?*

I looked up at Casey. She just smiled and continued. "When a person knows the reason they're here, they've identified their 'Purpose For Existing.' We call it 'PFE' for short. During someone's lifetime, they may find ten, twenty, or hundreds of things they want to do to fulfill their Purpose For Existing.

"As a matter of fact, our most fulfilled customers are the ones who don't just *know* their PFE. They also allow themselves to try all the activities they believe will fulfill it."

"And your least fulfilled customers?" I asked a little hesitantly.

"They do lots of things too," she said slowly.

I paused, waiting for her to say more. She didn't. Then it hit me. "They do lots of things which aren't part of their PFE, don't they?" I asked.

Casey nodded.

I sat in silence for a little while, thinking. "It seems so simple," I said, "but then at the same time it seems so confusing."

"What do you mean?" Casey asked.

"I don't know. Just the idea of figuring out what could help me fulfill my PFE…. That feels like a daunting task. I don't even know where I'd start."

She replied with a question. I was beginning to notice she did that a lot. "John, suppose you determine your Purpose For Existing is to build sports cars. And you decide you want to fulfill that PFE. What would you do?"

I thought for a moment. "I suppose I'd read a lot about sports cars. Maybe I'd visit a place where they build them, or contact some people who have built them in the past and get their advice. I guess I might try to get a job where they design or assemble sports cars."

Casey nodded, "Would you stay in one place? Talk to just one person?"

I paused and thought again. "No, I suppose if I really wanted to know how to build sports cars, I'd visit lots of different places and talk to lots of different people. That way I'd have a broader perspective."

I looked at her and shrugged, "I guess maybe it's not as daunting as it felt a moment ago. Maybe learning about what could fulfill my Purpose For Existing is as simple as exploring and getting exposure to different people and things related to it."

Casey nodded, "Exactly. We're all limited by our current experiences and knowledge. The important word there is *current*. More than ever before in human history, we have access to information, people, cultures, and experiences from all over the world.

"As we try to find what will fulfill our PFE, our limits today aren't really about accessibility. They're about the limitations we impose on ourselves."

I nodded, "You're right. You're totally right. And yet it seems like I don't take advantage of that accessibility very much. When I think of how I spend my time, it's pretty much the same thing every day."

"Why is that?" Casey asked.

I looked down at the menu.

Why are you here?

"I guess maybe it's because I don't know the answer to that," I said and pointed to the first question. "Without knowing exactly why I'm here, and what I want to do, I just do what most people are doing."

Casey didn't reply to that right away. Then she looked at me. "In your experience, has 'doing what most people are doing' helped you fulfill *your* Purpose For Existing?"

Twelve

Casey's question had my mind racing. *Has doing what most people are doing, helped me fulfill my Purpose For Existing?* Before I could answer, she spoke again.

"Have you ever seen a green sea turtle, John?"

"A sea turtle?"

"Correct. In particular, a big green sea turtle, with splotches on its flippers and head."

"I've seen pictures of them," I replied. "Why?"

"As strange as it may sound," Casey began, "I learned one of my most important life lessons about choosing the things I do each day, from a big green sea turtle."

"What did he tell you?" I asked, not at all successful in suppressing my smile.

"Funny," she answered, and smiled back. "He didn't specifically *tell* me anything, but he still taught me a lot.

"I was snorkeling off the coast of Hawaii," she began. "The day had already been spectacular, in that I'd seen a purple spotted eel and an octopus, both of which were new for me. There were also thousands and thousands of fish, representing every color you can imagine. From the most striking blue neon to incredible deep shades of red....

"I was about a hundred feet away from the beach, and diving down among some large rock structures. When I turned to my right, there was a large green sea turtle swimming next to me. That was the first time I'd ever seen one in the wild, so I was ecstatic. I rose to the surface, cleared my snorkel, and floated on top of the water, so I could watch him.

"He was right underneath me and moving away from shore. I decided I'd stay on the surface and swim with him for a while. To my surprise, although he appeared to be moving pretty slowly, sometimes paddling his flippers and other times just floating, I couldn't keep up with him.

"I was wearing fins, which gave me propulsion power through the water, and didn't have on a buoyancy vest or anything that would slow me down. Yet he kept moving farther from me, even though I was trying to keep up.

"After about ten minutes, he lost me. Tired, disappointed, and a little embarrassed I couldn't keep up with a turtle, I turned back and snorkeled to shore.

"The next day I returned to the same spot, with the hope of seeing more turtles. Sure enough, about thirty minutes after walking into the water, I turned to look at a school of tiny black and yellow fish, and there was another green sea turtle. I watched him for a while as he paddled around the coral.

"Then I tried to follow him as he swam away from the shore. Once again, I was surprised to find I couldn't keep up. When I realized he was pulling ahead of me, I stopped paddling and just floated and watched him. It was at that moment when he taught me the important life lesson."

Casey stopped speaking and just looked at me.

"Casey, you can't end the story there," I said with mock annoyance. "What did he teach you?"

She smiled, "I thought you were a nonbeliever in green sea turtles being able to tell you something?"

I smiled back, "I'm still doubtful on the *tell* part, but from the way the story is going, I'm starting to become a believer in the teaching possibilities. What happened next?"

She nodded, "Well, as I was floating on the surface, I realized something. When the turtle was swimming, it linked its movements to the movements of the water. When a wave was coming at him, he would float, and paddle just enough to hold his position. When the pull of the wave was from behind him though, he'd paddle faster, so that he was using the movement of the water to his advantage.

"The turtle never fought the waves. Instead, he used them. The reason I hadn't been able to keep up with him was because I was paddling all the time, no matter which way the water was flowing. At first this was fine, and I was able to stay with him. I even had to slow my paddling sometimes.

"But the more I battled against the incoming waves, the more tired I became. This meant that when the wave was going out, I didn't have enough energy to take advantage of it.

"As wave after wave came in and went out, I became more and more fatigued and less effective. Not the turtle though. He kept optimizing his movements with the movements of the water. That's why he was able to swim faster than I could."

"Casey," I began, "I think I appreciate a good turtle story..."

"Green sea turtle story," she interrupted me, and smiled.

"Right, *green sea turtle story*. I think I appreciate a good *green sea turtle story* as much as the next person. Maybe more actually, since I love the ocean." I paused, "But I'm not sure I understand how this relates to the way people choose what things will fill up their days."

Casey slowly shook her head, "And I had such high hopes for you," she said, and smiled again.

I rolled my eyes at her sarcasm. "Okay, okay," I replied. "Give me a minute."

Thirteen

I thought through what we'd been talking about before the green sea turtle story.

"You were saying," I began, "that once someone knows why they're here—they know their PFE—then they can spend their time on things that fulfill it. You were also saying that people who don't know their PFE, also spend their time on lots of things. That's when I deduced that what they spend their time on *doesn't* help them fulfill their PFE."

Casey nodded, "So far so reflective, and I think I sense a major insight just around the corner."

"Yes, you do," I replied, and smiled at her entertaining sarcasm. "I think the turtle—the green sea turtle—taught you that if you aren't in tune with what you want to do, you can waste your energy on lots of other things. Then when opportunities come your way for what you *do* want, you might not have the time or strength to spend on them."

She nodded, "Very nice. And I appreciate the catch on the 'green sea turtle' instead of just 'turtle.'" She paused a moment and became more serious. "It was a really big moment for me. Definitely one of my 'Aha' moments in life.

"Each day there are so many people trying to persuade you to spend your time and energy on them. Think about just your mail and email. If you were to participate in every activity, sale, and service offering you get notified of, you'd have no free time. And that's just mail and email. Add on all the people who want to capture your attention for television time, online activities, places to eat, travel destinations…."

She paused, "You can quickly find yourself living a life that's just a compilation of what everyone else is doing, or what people *want* you to be doing.

"When I got back to the beach after watching the turtle on the second day, I was filled with all these insights. I sat on my towel and wrote them in my journal. I realized that in my life, the incoming waves are made up of all the people, activities, and things that are trying to capture my attention, energy, and time but are *not* associated with my PFE.

"The outgoing waves are the people, activities, and things that can *help me* fulfill my PFE. So the more time and energy I waste on the incoming waves, the less I have for the outgoing ones.

"Once I had that picture in my head, it really put things in a different perspective. I became much more selective about how much 'paddling' I did, and for what reasons."

I nodded slowly, reflecting on her story and thinking about how I spent most of my time each day. "Interesting," I said. "I see what you meant by learning something from a green sea turtle."

Casey smiled and got up from the table. "I thought you might." She indicated toward my plates of food, "But I think I'm keeping you from eating your breakfast. Why don't I let you work on that for a while. I'll come back in a little bit and see how you're doing."

A thought suddenly flashed in my mind. "Casey, can I borrow a piece of paper and your pen before you go?"

"Sure." She took the pen out of her apron, ripped a piece of paper from her order pad, and put them both on the table.

She winked at me, "The answer will surprise you."

"How do you know—?" I started to ask, but she was already on her way to the kitchen.

I picked up the pen and started writing figures on

the paper. Average life expectancy of seventy-eight years...twenty-two years old when I graduated college...awake sixteen hours per day...twenty minutes each day spent on mail and e-mail....

When I finished all my computing, I couldn't believe the answer. I did the math again. Same answer.

I realized Casey wasn't kidding about the impact of the incoming waves. If from the time I graduated college until the time I was seventy-eight years old, I spent just twenty minutes per day opening and looking at mail and e-mail I didn't really care about—that used up well over a year of my life.

I rechecked my math a third time. It was true.

"Well?" It was Casey. She was walking from the kitchen to the other end of the cafe, but had paused when she saw me looking at the paper.

"You're right," I replied. "I am surprised. Actually, I think I'm beyond surprised and quickly heading to shocked. Do you realize that junk mail alone could eat up an entire year of your life?"

She smiled, "Not all mail and e-mail is junk, John."

"No, I get that, but a lot of it is. Besides, it's not just those things. I was sitting here wondering what other incoming wave items are occupying my time and energy every day. How many minutes am

I spending on *those*?"

"It can get you thinking," she said. "That's why my time with the green sea turtle made such a big impact on me."

Fourteen

Casey continued on to the other end of the cafe and I started working on the pancakes. They were as delicious as the other items had been. As I ate, I thought about my conversations with her and Mike. They were not your average cafe conversations. Why are you here? What do you do once you know why you're here? What can you learn from a green sea turtle?

A few minutes later, as I was making progress on the rest of the fruit, Mike came over.

"How's the food, John?"

"Terrific. This is some place. You know, you should really think of franchising. You could make a fortune."

Mike smiled, "Maybe I already have a fortune."

"Then why would you be working here...?" I began. I tried to stop myself, but it was already too late. I looked at him apologetically. "I'm sorry, Mike. I didn't mean this isn't a great place. I just meant…. I'm not sure what I meant, actually."

"That's okay," Mike said. "I've gotten that question more than once." He looked at me for a moment, "You ever hear the story of the businessman who went on vacation and met a fisherman?"

I shook my head, "I don't think so."

"Interested? It relates to your comment on franchising."

"Sure," I replied and gestured to the booth across from me. "Please, have a seat."

Mike nodded and sat down. "Well, the story goes that a businessman went on vacation to get away from it all. To 'recharge his batteries,' so to speak. He flew to this faraway location and wandered into a small village. Over the course of a few days, he watched the people in the community and noticed there was one fisherman in particular who seemed the happiest and most content of everyone. The businessman was curious about this, so one day he approached the fisherman and asked him what he did every day.

"The man replied that he woke up every morning and had breakfast with his wife and children. Then his kids would go off to school, he would go fishing, and his wife would paint. He would fish for a few hours, return with enough fish for the family meals, and then he'd take a nap. After dinner, he and his wife would take a walk along the beach and watch the sunset while the kids swam in the ocean.

"The businessman was stunned. 'You do this every day?' he asked.

"'Most days,' replied the fisherman. 'Sometimes we do other things, but for the most part, yes, this is my life.'

"'And every day you can catch fish?' asked the businessman.

"'Yes,' replied the fisherman. 'There are many fish.'

"'Can you catch more than just the fish you bring home for your family?' inquired the businessman.

"The fisherman looked at him, smiled, and replied, 'Oh yes, I often catch many more and just let them go. You see, I love fishing.'

"'Well, why don't you fish all day and catch as many as you can?' asked the businessman. 'Then you could sell the fish and make lots of money. Pretty soon you could buy a second boat, and then a third boat. Their fishermen could catch lots of fish too. In a few years you could have an office in a major city. As a matter of fact, I bet within ten years you could have an international fish distribution business.'

"The fisherman smiled again at the businessman.

'Why would I do all that?'

"'Well, for the money,' replied the businessman. 'You would do it so you could get a lot of money and then retire.'

"'And what would I do when I retired?' asked the fisherman, still smiling.

"'Well, whatever you want, I suppose,' replied the businessman.

"'For instance, maybe I could eat breakfast with my family?'

"'Yes, I guess so,' said the businessman, a little annoyed the fisherman wasn't more excited about his idea.

"'And if I wanted to, since I love fishing so much, I could fish a little bit each day?' the fisherman continued.

"'I don't see why not,' said the businessman. 'There probably won't be as many fish by then, but there should still be some.'

"'Then perhaps I could spend my evenings with my wife, walking along the beach and watching the sunset, while our children swim in the ocean?' inquired the fisherman.

"'Sure, whatever you want, although by then your kids will probably be grown,' said the businessman.

"The fisherman smiled at the other man, shook

his hand, and wished him well on his efforts to recharge."

Mike finished the story and looked at me. "What do you think, John?"

I paused for a moment, "I think I'm a little bit like the businessman. I spend most of my time working, so that I'll have enough money to retire."

Mike nodded, "I used to do that too. Then one day I came to a very important personal realization. In my mind, retirement was this time in the future when I'd have enough money to do what I wanted. The point at which I'd be free to participate in the activities I liked, and could spend every day in a way that fulfilled me.

"Then one evening, after a particularly unfulfilling day at work, I came to the conclusion there had to be a better way. Over time, I learned that somehow I'd gotten confused about how things *could* work. It was so simple it seemed crazy that I'd gotten it confused, but nonetheless I had."

I looked at Mike, "What did you figure out?"

"Well, I realized that for me, every day is an opportunity to fulfill the answer to the question you glimpsed on the back of the menu. Every day is a chance to do the things I want. I don't need to wait until 'retirement.'"

I put my fork down and sat back. I was a little

surprised at just how simple that sounded. "But that's so easy," I said. "If it's that easy, why doesn't everyone spend more time doing what they want?"

Mike smiled, "Well, I'm afraid I can't speak for everyone." He looked at me, "Are you spending a lot of time doing what you want?"

This wasn't the direction I expected the conversation to go. I was hoping Mike would keep doing the talking, and I could just listen. I thought about his question for a moment.

"No, not really," I replied.

"Why not?"

This was further progress down a path I hadn't anticipated. I shrugged, "To be honest, I'm not sure. I didn't really know what I wanted to study when I went to college. Eventually I made the decision to go into a program I kind of liked, and a lot of people said was good for getting a job after graduation. When school ended, I started working. Then my focus shifted more and more towards making money. Eventually I was earning a pretty good salary, and I just sort of settled into a pattern."

I paused for a moment, "I'm also not sure I ever thought about this question," I said, and pointed at the menu. "Not until tonight."

Mike nodded, "Like I mentioned earlier, it's kind of funny how and when it hits different people."

I shook my head a little, "This seems really crazy."

"What do you mean?"

"What we were just talking about. Why is it we spend so much of our time preparing for when we can do what we want, instead of just doing those things now?"

Mike nodded slowly, "There's someone here tonight who might be able to provide you with some insight into that one."

"Who?" I asked.

"Hang on a minute," Mike replied. He got up from the table and went to where Casey was talking with the other customers. I couldn't hear what they were discussing, but in a few moments one of them got up, and she and Mike began walking toward me.

Fifteen

When they reached my table, Mike introduced me to the woman he'd brought over. "John, I'd like you to meet a friend of mine. This is Anne." He looked at Anne, "And this is John. Tonight is his first time at the cafe."

I stood and Anne and I shook hands.

"Nice to meet you," I said. "I take it from Mike's introduction that you dine here a lot?"

She smiled, "Every once in a while. It's one of those places you just kind of find yourself at when you need it most."

I nodded, "I'm beginning to sense that."

"John and I were just discussing one of your favorite topics, Anne. I thought perhaps we could bring you in for an expert opinion."

She laughed, "Well, I'm not sure about the expert part, but I'm rarely short of an opinion. What were you talking about?"

"John was asking why we spend so much of our life preparing for when we can do what we want. Instead of just living that life now."

"Ah, that is one of my favorite topics," she said, and laughed again.

Anne's laugh was infectious, and I liked her immediately. "Please sit down, Anne. It would be great to hear your perspective. Yours too, Mike, if you can spare the time."

As we all sat down, Mike commented, "Before she begins, you should know a little about Anne. She has an advanced degree from the top marketing school in the world and was a highly acclaimed executive in the advertising world for many years."

"Wow," I replied. "That sounds very impressive."

"Not necessarily," Anne said and smiled, "but it's probably important for context." She paused a moment, looking at me. "John, do you ever watch television, read magazines, browse the web, listen to the radio…. Those kinds of things?"

"Sure," I replied. "Why?"

"Part of the answer to your question about why we spend so much time preparing to do what we want, instead of just doing it, lies in the messages that are placed in front of us every day," she said. "You see, advertisers have long known that if you effectively target people's fears, and their desire to be fulfilled, you can motivate them to do things. If you can play to the right fear, or to the right desire, you can get them to buy specific goods and use particular services."

I looked at her a little confused, "Can you give me an example?"

She nodded, "Have you ever seen or heard an advertisement where the content focused on enabling you to be happy or secure? Something where the message was, 'If you have this product, your life will be better?'"

"I suppose so," I replied.

"It's usually subtle," she commented. "Most of the time companies don't come right out and say it. But when you know what to look for, or when you've been involved with creating a lot of advertisements, you see it. The purpose of those messages is to get you to believe that you can achieve fulfillment through a particular product or service.

"For instance, driving *this* make of automobile will bring meaning to your life. Eating *that* brand of ice cream will translate into happiness. Having *this* type of diamond, will bring you contentment.

"And," she continued, "let me tell you something very important. An even more subtle, but more powerful message is usually conveyed. Not only will those products *enable* you to be fulfilled if you have them, but *not* having them can *keep you* from being fulfilled."

I looked at Anne quizzically. "So are you suggesting people shouldn't buy things? That seems kind of unrealistic."

She gently shook her head, "No, don't get me wrong. I'm not saying don't buy a car, eat ice-cream, or go to the mall. To the contrary, I firmly believe each person should do what they want in life.

"You asked why we spend so much time preparing for the life we want to live, instead of just living it. Part of the answer is if we aren't careful, we buy into the mass of marketing messages we're exposed to every day. We end up believing the answer to happiness and fulfillment lies in a product or service."

She shrugged, "Eventually, that can result in us putting ourselves in a financial position where we feel we *have to* keep doing things that aren't what we want."

I looked at her quizzically again, "I'm not sure I follow you."

"Let me give you a very general example," Anne replied. "Keep in mind that this doesn't apply to every person. It should help explain what we've been talking about, though."

Sixteen

"From a young age, we're exposed to advertisements conveying the message that fulfillment comes from *things*," Anne began. "So what do we do?"

I shrugged, "I guess we buy some items to see if the advertisements are true."

She nodded, "Exactly. The challenge though, is in order to buy those things, we need what?"

I shrugged again, "Money?"

"Right again," she said. "So to solve that problem, we get a job. It may not be our ideal job, and our time at work may not be exactly how we want to spend the hours of our life. Nonetheless, we take the job so we can pay for whatever we want to buy. We tell ourselves it's temporary. Soon we'll be doing something else, something more in line with what we really want to do.

"The problem is, because the job isn't fulfilling,

and because we spend so much time at it, we feel more and more unfulfilled. Meanwhile, all around us are people talking about how they can't wait for that day in the future when they'll retire and *then* do the things they want.

"Before long, we too start to envision this almost mystical future point. A time when we also won't have to do our job, and can instead live the life we want.

"In the meantime though, to offset the fact that we *aren't* spending every day doing what we want, we purchase more things. We hope in some small way the advertising messages are true. That those items will bring the fulfillment our daily life doesn't.

"Unfortunately, the more we purchase, the more bills we have. Therefore, we need to spend more time at work to pay for everything. Since time at our job isn't really the way we want to spend our life, this results in even more feelings of un-fulfillment. Because now, we have *even less* time for doing what we want."

"And so we buy more things," I said. "I think I see where this is going. It doesn't sound like a very positive cycle."

"Positive or not," Anne replied, "the end result is people keep working for a long time on activities that don't necessarily fulfill their PFE. Meanwhile, they keep looking to the future. That time when they don't have to work anymore, and can finally do what they really want."

Anne finished and we all sat in silence for a moment. "Wow," I eventually said. "I've never thought of it that way before." I looked from Anne to Mike and back at Anne again. "Are you sure about all this?"

They both laughed. "John, just as I wouldn't recommend taking advertising messages at face value, but for you to see them for what they really are, I wouldn't want you to simply accept anything I say," Anne replied. "Casey mentioned you were talking about how we all have the chance to expand our exposure to things—to give us a better perspective on all that's out there."

I nodded in reply.

"Well, what I've shared with you is just one person's opinion. Now that you've heard it, you can look at the world around you and decide if you think some, all, or none of it is true."

Seventeen

I reflected for a few moments on all Anne had said. Then I looked at her. "That example you gave earlier. Did you go through that cycle?"

She nodded, "Sadly, yes I did. I can laugh about it now. At the time though it definitely wasn't funny. I was really unhappy and felt like I'd lost control of my own life."

"In what way?" I asked.

She paused, "Well, back then I had what seemed like a very rational approach to life. 'I worked all weekend,' I'd say to myself. 'So I deserve a treat of a new outfit, the latest electronic gadget, or some new stylish home furnishing.'"

She looked at me, "The problem was, since I was always working, I rarely had time to use what I'd treated myself to. People would come over to my house and tell me how much they loved it, but I was seldom there enough to enjoy it.

"One night, after I'd gone through a large stack of bills that would once again eat up most of my income for the month, I fell back on my bed and stared up at the ceiling. It was all I could do not to break into tears. I realized life was passing me by. I was spending it at a job I didn't really care about, and trying to compensate myself by buying things I also didn't really care about.

"To compound the problem, my plan for getting back to what I wanted to be doing, required me to work until I was sixty years old, when I could retire." She paused and looked at me, "It was a miserable feeling."

"That seems like a very different mind-set than you have now," I replied. "What changed it?"

Anne nodded, "That evening, after staring at the ceiling and trying to figure out how I'd gotten myself in the situation I was in, I decided to go for a walk. I lived in a large city, and the streets were full of people. I kept looking at everyone I passed, wondering whether any of them felt the same way I did.

"Were *they* happy? Were *they* doing what they wanted? Were *they* feeling fulfilled? Eventually, I stopped in at a small coffee shop I'd seen a number of times, but never visited."

Anne glanced over at Mike and smiled, "To my surprise, an acquaintance of mine was sitting there. I'd met him on a few occasions and was impressed by how at ease he always seemed.

"He asked me to join him, and over three hours and many cups of coffee, we traded theories on life. When I explained my situation, he smiled and suggested that maybe I was reading too many of my own advertisements. I told him I wasn't sure what he meant, and he explained the cycle I described to you a few minutes ago. He went on to tell me something else. Something which has stuck with me ever since.

"'The challenge,' he explained, 'is to realize that something is fulfilling because *we* determine it's fulfilling. Not because someone else tells us it is.'"

"Wow," I said.

Anne glanced at Mike again and nodded, "Uh-huh. So that night when I got home, I sat and reflected on what was fulfilling for me—and why. I challenged myself to think about how I wanted to spend each day. Before long, I was asking myself *why* I wanted to spend my time in those ways. Eventually, that line of thinking led me to here."

I looked down. Anne was pointing at the menu. *Why are you here?*

"And then?" I asked.

Anne laughed, "Well, I think Casey probably

already explained to you that once you ask yourself 'Why am I here?' things change for you. I can tell you that ever since that night, I haven't been the same."

"Really?" I asked.

She nodded, "It started slowly, with me taking a little more time for myself each week. I stopped treating myself to 'things' as compensation for working so hard. Instead, the treat became spending time doing what I wanted. Each day I made sure I spent at least an hour doing something I really liked. Sometimes it was reading a novel I was excited about. Other days it was going for a long walk or playing sports.

"Eventually, the one hour became two, and that progressed to three. Before I knew it, I was totally focused on doing what I wanted to do. Things that fulfilled my answer to—'Why am I here?'"

Eighteen

Anne turned to Mike, "Have you and John had the death discussion yet?"

"The what?" I asked, surprised.

Anne smiled and pointed to the menu. "The second question."

I looked down.

Do you fear death?

I'd pretty much forgotten about the other two questions on the menu. With all I'd been exposed to with the first one, I wasn't sure I was ready to think about the rest.

"They're related," Mike commented.

There was that mind reading thing again. Just when I was starting to think this place was a normal cafe. Actually, I guess I never thought that.

"What do you mean, *related*?" I asked.

"Do you fear death?" Anne asked. "Most people

do. As a matter of fact, it's one of the most common fears people have."

I shrugged, "I don't know. I mean I don't want to die before I have a chance to experience what I want in life. But it's not like I'm thinking about death every day."

Anne looked at me, "People who haven't asked themselves the question you saw on the menu, and haven't taken steps to fulfill their PFE...." She paused, "Those people fear death."

It was my turn to pause. I looked at Anne and then Mike. "Are you saying most people spend part of every day thinking about death? I'm not sure I believe that. I mean I definitely don't."

Mike smiled and shook his head a little, "It's not quite like that, John. What we're talking about takes place primarily on the unconscious level." He hesitated a moment, "As each day passes, people intuitively know they're another day closer to not having a chance to do what they want in life. What they fear is that day that exists sometime in the future, when they'll no longer *have* the chance. They fear the day they'll die."

I reflected on that for a moment. "But it doesn't have to be like that, does it? I mean if someone asked themself why they're here. Then they chose what they wanted to do to fulfill their PFE. And then they actually did those things.... Why would they fear death? You can't fear not having the chance to do something if you've already done it. Or if you're doing it every day."

Anne looked at Mike, who nodded slightly, then back at me. She smiled, "No, you can't," she said softly. She reached across the table and put her hand on mine, "It's been a pleasure meeting you, John. I'm afraid I need to get back to my friend, but I've truly enjoyed our conversation."

"I have as well," I replied. "Thanks for sharing your story with me."

We all stood. Then Anne left the booth and started walking back to her table. I slid back into my seat. I felt different, somehow. Like I'd just learned something that was going to be very valuable for a long time.

Mike looked at me, "You all right, John? You look a little stunned."

I nodded, "Just thinking. What you and Anne were explaining makes a lot of sense. I'm surprised I haven't heard it before, or thought of it myself."

He smiled, "Everything in its own time, John. Maybe you did come across it before. But you just weren't ready back then."

Mike reached down and took two of the empty plates from the table. "Why don't I clear some of this away for you." He nodded toward the plate with the hash browns, "You still working on those?"

"Amazingly, yes," I replied, drawing myself out of my thoughts and back to the food in front of me. "They're too good to pass up, and I've still got a little room left."

As Mike walked away from the table, I reflected on everything he, Anne, and I had just discussed. It was a lot to take in. I thought about Anne's story and the impact of advertisements. How much of my definition of success, happiness, and fulfillment *had been* determined by people other than myself? That was hard to know. I decided that from now on, I'd try to be more aware of the messages behind what people were saying.

The discussion about death was something entirely different. I knew I'd come to a deeper level of understanding because of that conversation. It wasn't that I'd been living in a state of emotional despair, just worrying about death. It wasn't even something I thought about often. But the concept of living a life that fulfills my own purpose, and the impact that would have on how I viewed each day, resonated very well with me.

"You can't fear not having the chance to do something, if you've already done it, or you're doing it every day," I said to myself.

I wished I *had* thought of that sooner. "Still," I reflected, "it's not enough to know the concept. The point is to actually put it to use."

Nineteen

I looked down at the menu sitting in the middle of the table.

Why are you here?

Do you fear death?

Are you fulfilled?

The questions didn't seem nearly as odd compared to the first time I'd read them. Their importance was a lot more obvious now.

Are you fulfilled?

"Until you go beyond merely knowing why you're here, and actually start working towards it, I don't think you can be fulfilled," I thought to myself.

"But doing that isn't always so easy, is it?"

I looked up, startled. Casey smiled and proceeded to fill my water glass from the pitcher in her hand. I hadn't heard her approach the table. Like Mike earlier, it was like she'd appeared out of nowhere.

"No, no it isn't," I replied, trying to gather my thoughts. "I mean the job I have now is something I know how to do. I'm good at it. I get paid for it."

I hesitated, "What happens if I ask myself why I'm here, and when I figure out the answer, I don't know how to do those things? Or what if I can't get a job doing them? What will I do for money then? How will I pay my bills, or save for retirement?"

I shook my head, "Or what if I'm not good at whatever the new things are? Or if they're things other people laugh at, or don't respect?"

Casey nodded as I shared my fears. Then she looked at me, "John, do you think once a person goes through the steps to identify why they're here, and comes up with their true answer, they'll be excited about what they've discovered?"

I paused for a second, trying to envision what that would be like. "I would hope so," I replied. "If they've truly figured out why they exist, I'd think that's *very* exciting."

"Do you think it would be equally exciting to do what helps fulfill that reason?" she asked.

I paused again. The questions seemed too easy. "I must be missing something," I thought. "Sure," I replied. "Why wouldn't it be? A person should be more excited and passionate about that than anything else."

Casey nodded, "Then why are you thinking the person would fail?"

I looked at Casey, unsure how to respond.

"Have you ever met someone who was completely passionate about what they did every day?" she continued. "They seemed to be spending their time on something they truly enjoyed?"

I thought for a moment, "Not many. But I know a few people who fit that description."

"Are they good at what they do?" Casey asked.

"Well yeah," I replied a little sarcastically. "With all the time they spend on it, they should be good at it. I mean they read about it in their free time, watch shows and videos about it, go to conventions on it.... With all that exposure, they should be good at what they do."

"Don't they get tired of doing all that?" she asked.

"No," I replied, shaking my head. "They can't seem to get enough of it. It's like they get charged by doing it, and...." I stopped in mid-sentence.

Casey smiled at me. "Do they seem to have much trouble finding work?"

I paused and thought for a moment, "No. Not the people I know. They have so much knowledge about what they like to do, and are so passionate about it, that everyone always goes to them for advice. Everyone always wants them involved in their projects."

"I would imagine they're pretty positive and upbeat people," she said. "They probably don't need to get away from it all to get 'recharged.'"

I let Casey's comments sink in. It was an interesting way to look at things. What would life be like if I was always doing things I wanted to do? What if I was always spending my time on something I was passionate about?

"But how about the money?" I asked, after a moment. "Just because you're good at something, or really knowledgable about it, doesn't mean you automatically get paid a lot for it. You might be able to find work, but will it pay well?"

Twenty

I felt a little better about myself for having come up with that one. "After all," I continued, "who knows what kinds of things a person would consider fulfilling."

Casey nodded. "I see," she said slowly. "Well, let's think of a worst possible scenario regarding the money. A person could live a life where *every day* they do what they've identified as something that fulfills their Purpose For Existing. However, they don't make 'a lot' of money. My, that would be tragic.

"Imagine the consequences," she continued. "You could find yourself having lived your life in a way that always fulfilled your PFE. You could spend your entire life doing what *you* wanted to do, because you figured out why you are here." She paused, "But... you might reach the age of sixty-five and not have sufficient retirement savings.

"What to do then?" she asked, her voice filled with mock drama. "I guess you'd just have to keep on doing what you want to do. That could indeed be tragic."

I rolled my eyes a little and smiled, "Casey, you can be downright sarcastic when you want to be."

She smiled back, "I'm just trying to make sure I completely understand your line of thinking."

"I get it, I get it. It goes back to Mike's story about the fisherman. Why wait to do what you want, when you can do it right now."

"It's that, and something more," she replied. "Do you remember your conversation with Anne about why people buy things?"

I nodded, "Sure. She was saying for a lot of people, part of the reason they want more money is to buy more things. They hope what they buy fulfills them, since other aspects of their life, like their work, leave them unfulfilled. But if they aren't careful, it becomes a downward spiral. The more they spend, the more time they have to work at the unfulfilling job to pay for it."

I looked at Casey, but she didn't reply. I thought for a moment. It felt like I was missing something. "It has to do with the worst possible scenario, doesn't it?" I asked.

Casey nodded.

I thought some more. "I guess the first thing is that a person in the worst-case scenario could always choose to do something else."

Casey just nodded again.

"And, that is the worst-case scenario. Obviously there's a better scenario. A person could get paid *a lot* for doing what they want and that fulfills why they're here."

Casey nodded once more, still not saying anything.

I sat back and took a drink of water. I knew I still hadn't figured out what I was missing. I was just about to ask for a hint, when a thought struck me.

"Maybe the money becomes less relevant," I began. "I mean it would depend on the person and their circumstances, but…" I paused.

"But?" Casey asked.

I looked away for a moment. The pieces were all there. I just had to put them in the correct order. Then suddenly, it was right in front of me.

"Everything OK?" Casey asked with a smile.

"Part of the reason I work, is to make money," I began excitedly. "I need money to pay for what I buy. When I think about what those things really mean to me, I believe I'm a little bit like the people Anne and I were talking about.

"It's things to help me escape for a while. Things that help me unwind and make me feel better about

97

my surroundings.

"What I'm wondering, is how much of that would I feel the need to buy, if I didn't *have* the need to 'escape?' Or if I didn't *need* to 'unwind'? If I was doing what I wanted to be doing, there should be less to escape from, and probably not nearly as much stress to be unwound from either."

I looked at Casey with amazement, "I'm not saying I'd go live in a shack in the woods somewhere, but I think maybe the definition of 'a lot of money' varies based on how much someone is living a life that fulfills their PFE."

"So are you suggesting that people should stop wanting to have more money?" Casey asked.

"No," I replied, shaking my head. "I'm saying that for myself, I think if I figured out why I'm here, and I was doing what I determined would fulfill that—I'd probably be a lot less concerned about money than I am. That's all I'm trying to say."

Casey smiled and nodded. Then she got up from the table and picked up two of my empty plates. "Interesting thoughts, John."

I looked around the cafe. "Discovered in an interesting place."

Twenty-one

A few minutes later, Casey returned and sat down across from me again. "John, when I took your dishes to the kitchen, Mike reminded me about something you might find interesting. It relates to our discussion about the challenges people might face when they're trying to fulfill their PFE."

"You mean my question about how they make money?" I replied.

"That's part of it, and there's more."

I nodded, "I'd like to hear it."

"For this to work," she began, "I need you to think about some of the people we were discussing earlier."

"You mean the ones I know who are completely passionate about what they're doing?" I asked. "The ones who seem to spend each day doing what they truly enjoy?"

She nodded, "Those are the ones. Did you notice anything about them?"

"Well, one woman was doing sales in a..."

"Actually," Casey interjected, "think more broadly than what they were doing. What did you notice *overall* about them?"

I sat back and closed my eyes for a moment, picturing the people in my mind. Then I looked at Casey again. "Well, as I mentioned before, they all seem genuinely happy. They appear to enjoy what they're doing. They're also really confident. It doesn't come across as false bravado either. They just seem to know things will go the way they want them to."

I paused, "This might sound strange, but another characteristic is they're all lucky. I mean, good things just happen for them. Unexpected things."

"For example?" Casey asked.

"Well, there's this one woman I'm thinking of. She's in advertising, which seems a little strange after my earlier conversation with Anne. Anyway, she was trying to land a big account. I don't even know what it was for anymore, but I do remember it was a big deal and a lot of other people had tried for it and failed.

"Well, she decided she wanted to land it. About two weeks into working on her presentation, she received a call from an old college friend. The two hadn't spoken in a long time. While they were catching up, they got on the topic of work, and the woman mentioned how she was trying to land this account. It turned out that the college friend, had another friend, who worked at the very company the woman was going after.

"A few phone calls later, the three of them met for dinner. Sure enough, a few weeks after that, the woman got the account." I shrugged, "That's what I mean by unexpected things happening for them. Those people just seem to be very lucky."

"Why do you think that is?" Casey asked.

I thought for a moment, "I don't know exactly. Maybe it's just coincidence. The funny thing is though, you asked me to think about the people who truly enjoy what they're doing. They're the ones spending time on things that seem to be in line with their PFE. These types of lucky events seems to happen all the time for those people."

Casey smiled and looked at me. "Does it only happen for those people? Have *you* ever experienced something like that?"

I sat back against the seat of my booth. "I suppose I have. I mean, I can't think of a particular instance off the top of my head, but I know there have been times when I was amazed at how something unexpected happened, just when I needed it to."

Casey nodded, "John, if you were able to remember those specific instances, I have a hunch you'd find a common link between them."

"Like maybe those were times when I was doing exactly what *I* wanted to be doing?" I asked.

Twenty-two

As I said the words, I felt a shudder run through me. It was the same feeling I'd had earlier, when it seemed like I learned something significant about myself.

Casey smiled, "I can't speak for you specifically, John, but in working here at the cafe, I've noticed some things about people in general. The ones who know their PFE, and are doing what they want to fulfill it, do seem very lucky. Unexpected, seemingly random things happen for them just when they need it most.

"I've asked some of them about it, and while they all agree it exists, not too many have the same opinion about what might cause it. To be honest, most of them aren't really concerned with identifying exactly what it is. They know it comes into play when they're fulfilling their Purpose For Existing, and they just see it as part of the way things work."

"Strange," I replied. "It sounds a little mystical."

She nodded, "Some people have said that. Others see it as part of the natural flow of the universe, or a higher power at work. Still others just view it as good luck. But they all agree it's there and is a factor in what they do."

I paused, "What do you think it is, Casey?"

She thought for a moment. "Honestly, I don't know for sure. I suppose it's all those reasons and maybe one other. Have you ever heard of the theory of exponential numbers?"

I shook my head, "I don't think so."

"It's pretty easy to understand. I'll give you an example. Imagine you tell someone something, and you can get them to tell other people. Then those other people tell still more people. Before long, your message has reached a far wider audience than you personally talked to."

"Kind of like passing along an e-mail or text," I said. "Where you send it to ten people, and they send it to ten more, and it keeps on going."

She nodded, "Exactly. It's the same concept. Only now, suppose you're letting people know about something you're trying to do which will help you fulfill your PFE. First, you share it with ten people. Then they each share it with ten more. Then those people keep sharing it, and on it goes. Before long, you have a whole bunch of people who know about your situation, and who potentially will help you."

I thought for a moment. "But why would those other people be willing to help me? And what would motivate them to talk with others about what I'm trying to do?"

Casey looked at me but didn't respond. I got the impression this was another one of those times when I was supposed to answer my own question. I sat, thinking for a few moments, but the solution wasn't coming to me. "I'm not sure I get it, Casey. How about a hint?"

"John, remember those people you thought of when we started this conversation—the ones who are working to fulfill their PFEs? How does it feel when you interact with them?"

"It feels great. You can't help but get caught up in their passion and enthusiasm for what they're doing. You just feel like you want to help."

I paused, "Oh come on, Casey. Are you telling me *that's* the answer? But how does that apply to the message being passed along?"

"John, you just said their passion and enthusiasm makes you feel like you want to help. If *you* couldn't help, but you knew others who might be able to, would you contact them?"

"Sure. You feel inspired to because they seem so..." I paused, looking for the right words.

"On the right path?" Casey asked.

I nodded, "Yeah, something like that. They seem so on the right path, you just want to help."

"And when you talk about them to other people who might be able to help, how do you speak of them?"

I smiled, half to myself, and half to Casey. "I speak with some of the same passion and enthusiasm as when they originally spoke to me. It's catching, and almost as if the emotion stays with the story, or with the need."

Casey shrugged, "Maybe that's your answer." She stood and gathered the remaining dishes from the table. "I'm impressed, John," she commented, holding the empty plates. "You must have been really hungry."

"It's the food," I replied. "It's too good to pass up."

I glanced at the kitchen and saw Mike. He waved. I waved back, feeling a little less self-conscious this time about the whole waving to cooks in a diner concept. "Casey, I don't suppose there's still a piece of that strawberry-rhubarb pie left?"

She laughed. "I'll head back to the kitchen and see what I can do."

Twenty-three

A few minutes later, Mike arrived at the table. "One piece of strawberry-rhubarb pie?" he asked.

On the plate in his hand was a piece large enough for three people. I smiled, "Mike, that looks like almost half the pie. I'm not sure I can handle all that."

He set an extra napkin and a new fork down on the table, along with the plate. "Take your time, no hurry. How was your discussion with Casey?"

"Interesting. Very interesting."

I pointed to the menu, "We were talking about people who seem to have answered the personal version of this first question," I said.

For a moment, the words on the menu transformed to *"Why am I here?"* and then slowly returned to *"Why are you here?"* I didn't even bother mentioning the change.

"Right, that one," I continued. "Those people seem to have some common characteristics. They know why they're here, they've figured out what they want to do to fulfill that reason, and they're completely confident they'll be able to do those things. And when they try to do them, events occur to help them succeed. Casey was explaining to me some of the theories people have on that last part."

Mike grinned, "There's a lot of speculation about that one. There has been for a long time, possibly back to the oldest philosophers."

"Mike, I'm a little confused about something. Why doesn't everyone go after their PFE? And before you start, I know I should ask that question of myself, and I was doing so when you walked up. But I'm wondering if there's a bigger, more encompassing reason than any I personally might have."

Mike put the mug he was holding onto the table across from me and slid into his side of the booth. "Certainly each of us has our own reasons," he began. "And those reasons are something every person has to address themselves, since they're unique to their own situation. There are some bigger items that seem to dominate, though."

"For example?" I asked, and took a big forkful of pie.

"Well, for many people it's as simple as never having been exposed to the concept of a Purpose For Existing. Others understand the concept, but aren't sure *they* have a PFE. Then there's some people who because of their upbringing or environment, don't believe they have the right to try and fulfill their PFE."

He paused, "Even people who feel they have a Purpose For Existing, and do believe they have the right to fulfill it, sometimes don't believe fulfilling it is as simple as knowing they can, and then doing what they want."

He shrugged, "This goes back to some of what you and Anne were talking about. Many people make their living and get their power by convincing others that they, or something they make or sell, are the key to fulfillment. Imagine if people came to the realization that we each control our *own* level of fulfillment.

"The people trying to convince others would lose their power. And for those types of people…," he paused, "they don't like that at all."

"That reminds me of one of the conversations Casey and I had earlier tonight," I said. "She helped me understand that once someone knows their PFE, they get to do and become whatever they want. They don't need someone else's permission or consent."

Mike nodded, "Correct. And on top of that, no one can keep a person from, or enable them to, achieve and do all they want in life. We each control our own destiny."

I thought about that, and on my earlier conversations with Casey and Anne. "What you're describing is very different from the messages I see and hear in my every-day life. I understand why it's so hard for people to even be exposed to the concepts of identifying why they exist and of controlling their own destiny. Let alone taking the next steps and actually living that way."

"Absolutely," Mike replied. "But it's not impossible. As a matter of fact, a couple of weeks ago a visitor to the cafe told Casey and me an interesting story about what *he* learned regarding controlling his own destiny."

"I'd love to hear that," I replied. "Does it involve more fishermen?"

Mike laughed, "Not this time, but it does involve sports. For years this guy had a recurring dream where he was standing over a very tough golf shot. As he explained it, he isn't a very good golfer when he's awake, so to face this challenge while sleeping was particularly frustrating. In his dream, the ball he needed to hit was sitting on a window ledge, a large down-sloping rock, or someplace equally ridiculous

and challenging.

"He'd try and try to plant his feet and get a good practice swing. But it never felt right and he knew his shot would be poor. The more practice swings he took, the more anxious and stressed he became.

"As his frustration peaked, he'd finally feel like he was ready to take the shot. However, as he started his back swing, the location of the ball would change, and he'd be faced with a new, equally challenging lie. He would then go through another buildup of stress and anxiety. This cycle kept repeating until he'd finally wake up with his heart pounding and his body full of stress."

"That sounds horrible," I commented.

Mike nodded, "He said it was. But then one night as he was having the dream, at the point where he typically reached his maximum level of frustration, he suddenly became aware he could just pick up the ball and put it somewhere else. Nothing was at stake, and he was the only one who really cared where he hit the ball from.

"He said he woke up with an incredibly strong sense of having gained a major insight into something that once he knew it seemed so obvious, but hadn't before. We ended our conversation with him explaining to me that,

'Despite what we may be taught to believe, are exposed

to in advertisements, or feel when we're stressed out at work, we each control every moment of our lives. I had forgotten that, and was trying to adjust to all kinds of other influences, as I was letting them control my existence.

'Just like no one really cared about where I hit the golf ball from except me, in life only you truly know what you want from your existence. Don't ever let things or people drive you to the point where you feel you no longer have control over your own destiny. Be active in choosing your path, or it will be chosen for you. Just move the golf ball.'"

Mike finished the story and looked at me. "See, no fishermen."

I smiled, "No fishermen indeed. A great story nonetheless. I like the message in there."

Mike nodded, "So did the guy. He said the message in the dream changed his life. From that point on, he realized he was in charge of choosing his own destiny. Now, whenever he encounters something and isn't sure what to do, he just tells himself—*move the golf ball*. He said merely speaking those words reminds him to do what he wants and not be afraid."

Twenty-four

I looked at my watch. It was a little after five in the morning. "I can't believe it," I said. "It's almost time to order breakfast again."

Mike smiled, "First you might want to finish off your pie."

"With pleasure," I replied, and grabbed another forkful. "It's delicious."

I chewed the bite and took a drink of water. "Mike, there's something I'm still unsure of. I've talked about it with both you and Casey, but I don't have the answer yet."

Mike nodded, "Ask away. Unless it's for the pie recipe. That's one of the few pieces of information we keep secret here. It was my mom's and I promised her I'd never give it away."

I grinned, "That's a shame, because it's truly amazing. But I understand. Luckily, I'm looking for a different answer."

"Which is?"

"Well, you and I have talked about people asking themselves, 'Why am I here?'" I began. "And Casey and I discussed the consequences of asking that question, and also what people can do when they know the answer. What I still don't know is..."

"How you go about finding the answer?" Mike interjected.

I nodded, "Right."

"I think for that one I better call Casey over. She and I combined can probably give you a better explanation than just one of us." Mike got up from the table and walked to the far end of the restaurant. Casey was sitting there, talking with Anne and her friend. I wondered if they were discussing some of the same things I was.

A moment later, Casey and Mike walked back to me.

"How's the pie?" Casey asked as the two of them sat down.

"Amazing," I said with a grin. "I'm almost full."

"Casey, John was asking how someone finds their answer to the first question," Mike said. He pointed to the *Why are you here?* on the back of the menu, which transformed into *Why am I here?* "I thought maybe both of us could try and answer his

115

questions."

Casey nodded, then looked directly into my eyes. In a very serious voice she asked, "Do you have a mailbox, John?"

"Sure," I replied, a little puzzled by her question.

"Well, on the first full moon that falls on the seventh day of the month after you've asked the question, a package will arrive in your mailbox. In that package is a document, which if held over a candle, will display a hidden message from those who know the answer. The message can only be read once in your life, only by candlelight, and has to be read on the seventh."

Casey's intensity was surprising me. I leaned forward to make sure I caught all the details she was explaining.

"When you open the package, you'll know it's the correct one, because the ribbon will be red, and tied in a double knot, with the..."

Suddenly, I felt the table begin to move—like it was vibrating with energy. I sat back, quickly.

"What's going on, Casey?" I asked, surprised. "The table..."

Casey continued on, as if she didn't notice anything. "...with the larger loop at least two times bigger than the smaller loop, and located in the upper left-hand corner of the package."

I looked over at Mike to see if he was feeling the vibrations too. To my surprise, and slight embarrassment, it was quickly clear from his demeanor that the table shaking was not a sign from the netherworld, as I had begun to think.

He'd been listening to Casey, and to contain his laughter, had put his hand over his mouth and leaned on the table. He was laughing so hard his whole body was shaking, and in turn it was causing the table to shake.

I rolled my eyes and smiled.

Casey turned to Mike and playfully punched him in the shoulder. "You're not a very good accomplice," she said.

"I'm sorry," he replied, laughing. "You were just *too* convincing. I couldn't contain myself."

"Okay," Casey said, "so I might have been taking a little bit of creative license regarding the answer to your question, John."

"A little bit!" Mike commented and smiled. "That was more like downright fabrication." He started to imitate Casey's voice, "*tied in a double knot, with...*"

We all started laughing.

"You're quite a storyteller, Casey," I said after a few moments. "However, I'm afraid you still haven't answered my question."

"In addition to having a little fun," she replied

with a smile, "I was trying to make a point. For some people, they ask the question, and want to know the answer, but they want someone or something else to be responsible for *bringing* them the answer."

"In a package that arrives on the seventh," I interjected, and smiled.

Casey nodded, smiling back, "Exactly. The thing is though, just as we have free will to decide what to do once we know the answer, we're also the one in control of *finding* the answer."

"So what you're saying," I began, "is you can't just take the first step and then wait around. If someone really wants to know why they're here, it's up to them to figure it out."

Mike nodded, "Exactly. And people do that in different ways. Some spend time meditating on why they're here. Others listen to their favorite music and note where their mind takes them. Many people take time alone in a natural environment. Others talk with friends and strangers about it. Some people are guided to their answer through ideas and stories they read in books."

"Which one works best?" I asked.

Casey turned to me, "It really depends on the person, John. Because we're the only ones who can determine what *our* answer is though, a lot of people do spend at least some time by themselves while they're seeking it."

"I can understand that," I replied. "It's hard to focus on something that important, when you're being bombarded with all kinds of other information and messages."

"Right," Mike added. "When people take time to meditate or be alone in a natural environment, they're usually trying to get away from the external 'noise,' so they can focus on what *they* really think."

"Is that all there is to it?" I asked.

Casey shook her head. "Not completely. Do you remember when we were talking about the value of getting exposure to various ideas, people, cultures, perspectives…?"

"Sure," I replied. "Our conversation about learning the different things someone could do to fulfill their Purpose For Existing."

Casey nodded, "Exactly. The same idea applies to people trying to figure out what their PFE is. Some find that when they experience new things and learn new ideas, certain ones resonate with them. Many people actually experience a physical reaction.

"They get goosebumps, a tremor up their spine, or they cry tears of joy when they come across something they really relate to. For others, a sense of knowing comes over them. Those can all be clues to help people identify their answer to why they're here."

"I can relate to what you're describing," I said. "I've had that happen before, when I read or heard something and just knew it was right for me." I smiled, "As a matter of fact, I've had a few of those moments tonight."

Casey smiled back, "Did we answer your question, John?"

I nodded, "You did. Thanks."

She got up from the table. "In that case, I'm going to check on our other guests. Is there anything else you need, John?"

I shook my head, "I don't think so. Unless I receive an unexpected package with red ribbon, delivered after a full moon.... Then I'll probably have a few more questions."

Casey laughed and winked at Mike, "Fair enough. You let us know."

Twenty-five

Mike and I sat in silence for a few moments after Casey walked away. Then he turned to me.

"John, where were you heading when you stopped in here?"

"I was starting my vacation. I felt like I needed some time away from everything." I paused, "An opportunity to think, I guess. Even though I didn't really know what I wanted to think about."

I glanced at my watch, "I have to say, in the last eight hours I've gotten some pretty good ideas for that, though."

He smiled and nodded in reply.

"Mike, do you mind if I ask you something personal?"

"Not at all. What is it?"

I looked at him. "What made *you* ask the question on the menu?"

He sat back and a smile crept onto his face. "What makes you so sure I have?"

"You, your demeanor, this place. I *don't* know for sure. But I get the feeling you're doing exactly what you want to be doing. I assume you asked the question at some point, and this place is the result."

Mike nodded slowly, "A number of years ago I was living a pretty hectic life. I was going to graduate school at night, working full time during the day, and filling every other minute training for and trying to make it as a professional athlete. For two-and-a-half years, almost every moment of my life was scheduled.

"When I graduated, I quit my job and took the summer off. I'd already lined up a new position which would start in the fall, so a buddy of mine and I decided to head down to Costa Rica. He'd just finished school too.

"We spent a month traveling around the country, hiking through rain forests, seeing wildlife, and getting immersed in a new culture. It was awesome. Inspiring on countless levels, and just tons of carefree fun, too.

"Then one day we were sitting on a log, eating fresh mangos and watching the waves crash against this unbelievably beautiful beach. We'd spent the afternoon bodysurfing perfect waves in water so warm, it felt like bathwater. And as the day wound

down, we were relaxing and watching the sky turn from brilliant blue, to pink, orange, and red, as the sun began to set."

"That sounds pretty spectacular," I said.

He nodded, "It was. And I remember looking out at it all and coming to the realization that while I had been planning every minute of my life for the last two-and-a-half years, this scene had been repeating itself every day.

"Paradise had been just a few hours' plane flight and some dirt roads away, and I didn't even know it existed. And I realized, not only had it existed for the two-and-a-half years I'd been so busy, but the sun had been setting there, and the waves had been crashing upon that beach, for millions if not billions of years."

He paused for a moment, "As those thoughts washed over me, I felt very small. My problems, the things I'd stressed about, my worries about the future, all seemed completely unimportant. I realized no matter what I did or didn't do during my life, whether my decisions were right, wrong, or somewhere in the middle, all of this would still be going on long after I was no longer alive.

"So I sat there, faced with the unbelievable beauty and grandeur of nature and the realization that my life was an infinitesimal piece of something much bigger. Then I was struck by the thought, *so why am I here? If all the things I thought were so important really aren't, then what is? What is my purpose for existing? Why am I here?"*

Mike looked at me and smiled, "Once I had those questions in my head, I went through something similar to what Casey described to you. They were always with me until I figured out the answers."

I sat back in my seat. I hadn't realized it, but as Mike was speaking, I was leaning forward to catch every part of what he was saying.

"Thanks, Mike. That's an amazing story."

He nodded, "The thing is, John, life is an amazing story. It's just that sometimes we forget we're the author, and we can write it however we want."

We sat in silence for a few moments, then Mike got up from the table. "I'm going to head back and start cleaning up the kitchen a bit. You need anything else?"

I shook my head, "No, I think I'm going to hit the road pretty soon. Speaking of which, I was pretty lost when I found this place. I don't really know which direction I'm supposed to go now."

Mike smiled. "Well, that depends...."

He started to say something else, and then paused as if he'd decided against it. When he spoke again, it was obviously on a different thought. "If you

125

continue on for a few miles down this road, you'll come to a four-way intersection. Take a right, and that will get you back to the highway. There's a gas station just before the entrance ramp. You've got enough gas to make it there."

I didn't know how he knew I'd be able to make it to the station, but I had a hunch he'd end up being right. I stood up from the table and extended my hand. "Thanks, Mike. You've got a very special place here."

He smiled and we shook hands, "You're welcome, John. Good luck with everything." And with that, he turned and walked away.

Twenty-six

I sat back down and my eyes were once again drawn to the menu sitting on the table.

Why are you here?

Do you fear death?

Are you fulfilled?

If someone had asked me those questions a day earlier, I'd have thought that person was a little out of it. Now, I couldn't imagine not having been exposed to them.

Casey came by, put down my check, and handed me a container. "It's the last piece of strawberry-rhubarb pie," she said and smiled. "A parting gift from Mike."

"And this is from me," she said, and handed me a menu. On the front, under the words "The Cafe of Questions," Casey had written a message. I read it, then read it again.

"A little something to remember us by," she added and smiled once more.

I nodded and looked up at her, "Thank you, Casey. Thank you for everything."

"My pleasure, John. That's what we are here for."

I sat in my booth for a few minutes after Casey left, just taking it all in. Then I got up, put some money on the table, and took the menu and container of pie.

I walked out of the cafe into the beginning of a new day. The sun had just begun to rise above the trees in the field across from the gravel parking lot. The air held both the last remnants of stillness that precede the start of a new day, and at the same time, the sounds of a day already in motion.

I felt refreshed and alive. I shifted the container I was carrying from my right hand to my left, and opened the door to my car.

"Why am I here?" I thought to myself. *"Why am I here?"*

It was indeed, a very new day.

Epilogue

After my night in the cafe, things changed for me. They weren't lightning-bolt-from-the-sky-type changes in terms of how they presented themselves. They were at least that dynamic in their eventual impact on my life, though.

Like Anne, I started slowly. I left the cafe wondering, "Why am I here?" and continued to ponder that question for the rest of my time off. The answers didn't all come right away. I learned that finding my Purpose For Existing, or PFE, as Casey called it, required more than just spending a vacation thinking about it, and then returning to everything I'd been doing. Like most things worth knowing, it took some effort to uncover the answer.

It was a combination of methods I learned from Casey and Anne which eventually enabled me to figure it out. I started by dedicating a small amount of time each day to doing things I liked. This was similar to the technique Anne had used. Then I tried to take advantage of the opportunities Casey talked about, and sought chances to learn and try new things. This helped me expand my universe of possible reasons for why I'm here.

Eventually, my PFE, and the ways I want to fulfill it, became clear. Ironically, that was when I faced the most difficult challenge of all. When you weigh two choices, and one is living a life that fulfills your Purpose For Existing, and the other is just living, you would think the decision is simple.

It isn't.

Over time, I've observed that this is the place where most people end their journey. They peer through a hole in the fence, and can clearly see the life they'd like to have. But for any number of reasons, they don't open the gate and walk into that life.

Initially, this caused me a great deal of sorrow. But as Mike said, and I have come to believe, people make that choice at all different times in their lives. Some when they're children, some later, and some never do. It can't be rushed, and it can't be anyone's decision but theirs.

For me, the knowledge that "you can't fear not having the chance to do something if you've already done it, or are doing it every day," helped me push open that gate. It's now one of the principles by which I live my life.

Not a day goes by when I don't think of something associated with the cafe. I'm reminded of Casey and her story of the green sea turtle every time I open my inbox and see it filled with advertisements and offers for things I don't need. That incoming wave is always present, ready to sap my time and energy. But now I know it exists, and I save my strength for the outgoing waves.

I also often think of Mike's story of sitting on the beach in Costa Rica. Viewed from a big picture perspective, our stresses, anxieties, victories, and losses account for little.

Yet it's in the face of our seeming insignificance, that we find meaning.

If I have any regret about making the changes I've made in my life, it's only that I didn't make them sooner. I guess I just wasn't ready before that night in the cafe.

Now, having sought out why I'm here, and living my life to fulfill that reason, I would never go back to a life on the other side of the gate.

Thank you for visiting

The Cafe On the Edge of the World

In addition to his books, John has
written a series of articles which he
makes available for cafe fans.

Those are available for download at

www.johnstrelecky.com/articles/

About the Author

Following a life changing event when he was thirty-three years old, John was inspired to sit down and tell the story of *The Cafe On the Edge of the World*.

Within a year after its release, word of mouth support from readers had spread the book across the globe—inspiring people on every continent, including Antarctica. It went on to become a seven time Best Seller of the Year, and has been translated into forty-three languages.

All of which continues to humble and amaze him. John's books have sold more than seven million copies and include, *Life Safari, The Big Five for Life, The Big Five for Life Continued, Ahas!- Moments of Inspired Thought* and *What I've Learned - Reflections on Living a Fulfilled Life*.

When he's not writing, John is often out traveling. His family's longest adventure was a year long backpacking trip around the world.

To contact John, please visit;
www.johnstrelecky.com

or via social media;
Facebook - @JohnStrelecky
Instagram - @JohnStrelecky
Twitter - @JohnStrelecky
LinkedIn - @JohnStrelecky